Why We Stand

DEDICATED TO MY BOYS
LIAM, MADDOX, AND ASHER KRUEGER.

TRY TO FIND ALL 22 FEATHERS!

Copyright 2023 by Real Patriot Publishing, LLC
All rights reserved.

Why We Stand

By Dillon Krueger

Suddenly, all the people stand up! They remove their hats and place their right hand over their hearts as they gaze at the American Flag.

A man on the field sings a song, then everyone cheers, and the game begins.

"WHAT WAS THAT SONG?" GEORGIE ASKS HIS DAD.

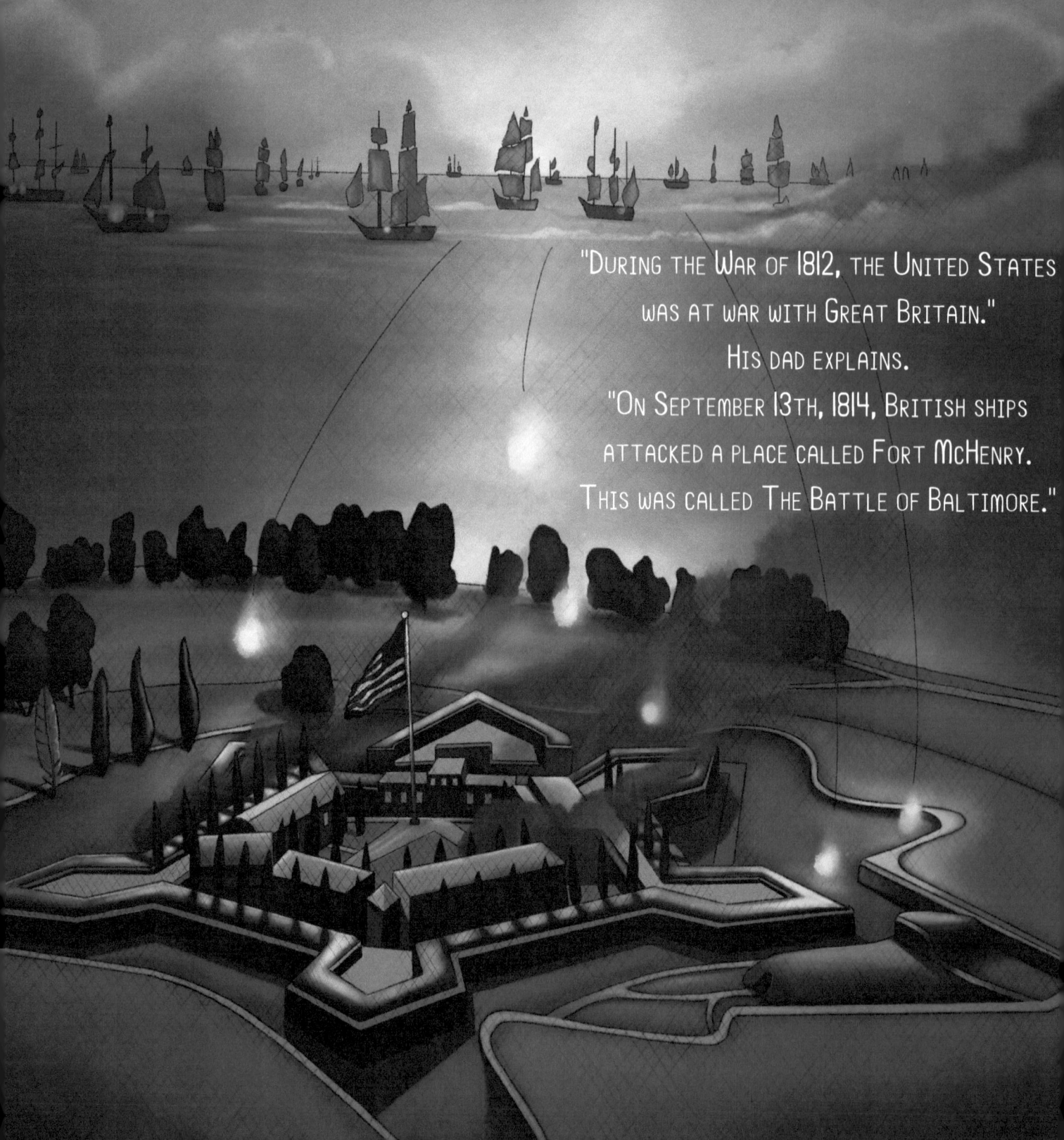

"The morning after, Key saw the American flag was still waving from Fort McHenry. He knew the Americans never surrendered and was inspired to write the Star-Spangled Banner. It became our National Anthem on March 3rd, 1931 and we have been playing it before sporting events since World War II."

"But why do we stand for the National Anthem?" asks Georgie.

"Isn't everyplace free?" asks Georgie.

"No son. We are very fortunate to be Americans." Responds his dad. "Many people want to come here to live the American dream."

"We are all equal. With enough hard work, every citizen can achieve their dreams!"

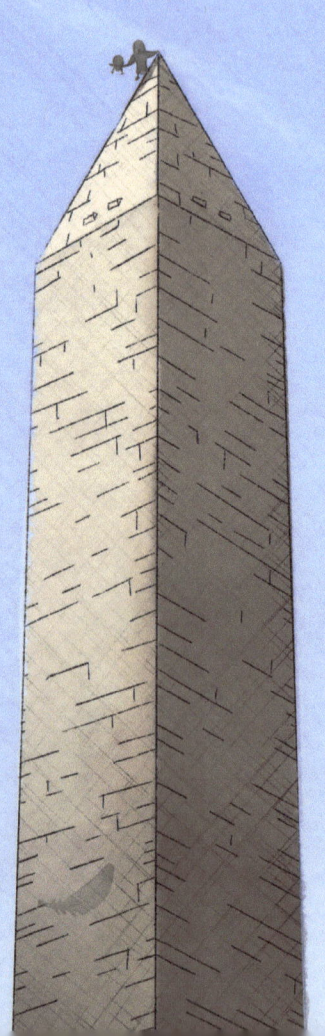

"So, why do we stand for the National Anthem?" Georgie ask again.

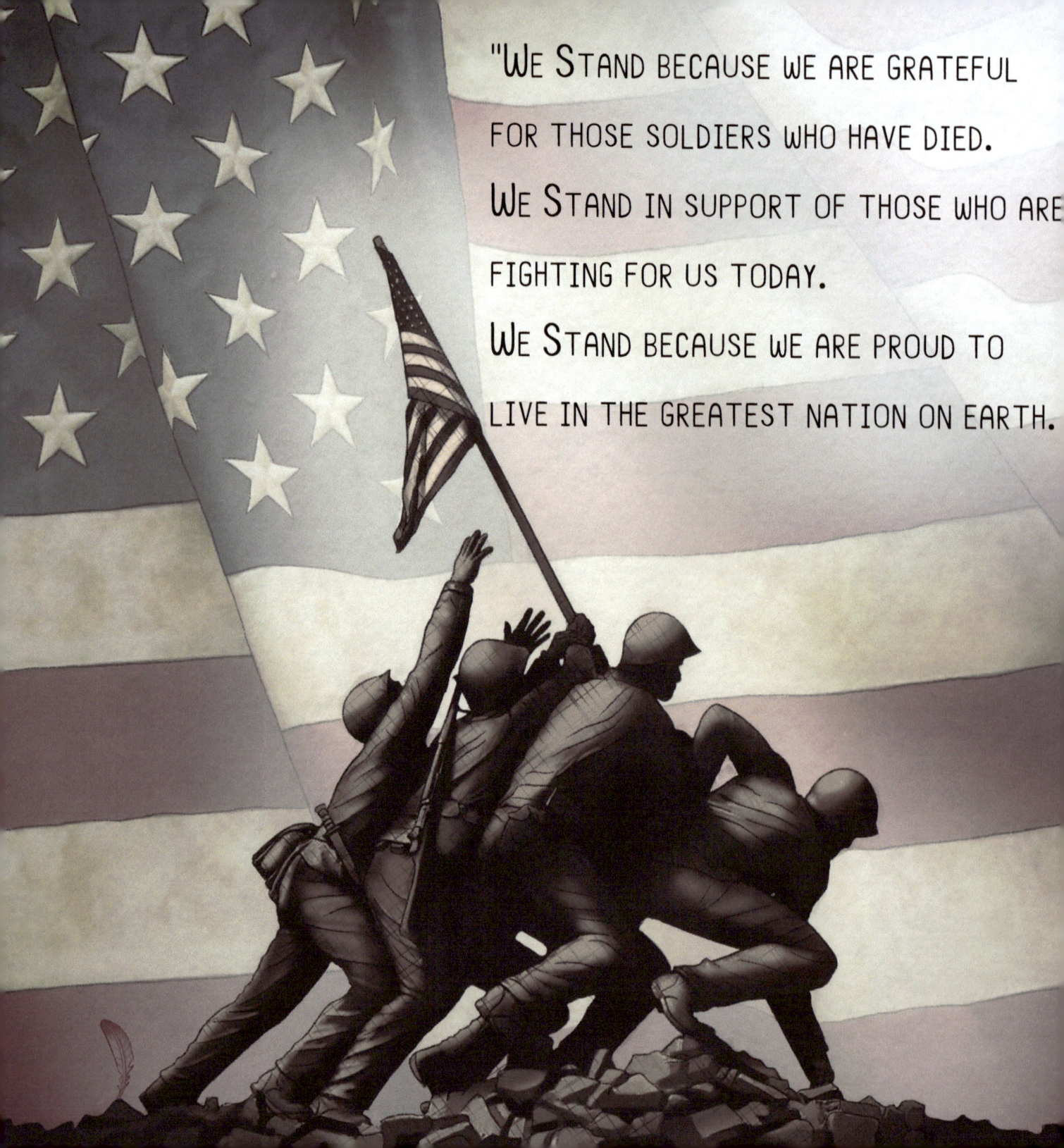

"We Stand Because We Are Free!"

"O say can you see, by the dawn's early light,

What so proudly we hail'd at the twilight's last gleaming,

Whose broad stripes and bright stars through the perilous fight

O'er the ramparts we watch'd were so gallantly streaming?

And the rocket's red glare, the bombs bursting in air,

Gave proof through the night that our flag was still there,

O say does that star spangled-banner yet wave

O'er the land of the free and the home of the brave?"

Follow Real Patriot Publishing for more great patriotic content!

INSTAGRAM

FACEBOOK

YOUTUBE

www.ingramcontent.com/pod-product-compliance
Lightning Source LLC
Chambersburg PA
CBHW040724060526
44119CB00083B/315